REPUBLIC RESTORED—
FAITH, FIDELITY,
AND ACTION

Republic Restored— Faith, Fidelity, and Action

Jeffrey Ziegler

Library of Congress Control Number:		2010913382
ISBN:	Hardcover	978-1-4535-7409-6
	Softcover	978-1-4535-7408-9
	Ebook	978-1-4535-7410-2

To order additional copies of this book, contact:
Xlibris Corporation
1-888-795-4274
www.Xlibris.com
Orders@Xlibris.com
84529

TABLE OF CONTENTS

Introduction

The character of America has been forged not through the victory of one political faction over another. Instead, our God-ordained national being has been formed through the celebration of freedom birthed in the fires of The Revolution and subsequently nurtured to maturity by the ratification of The Federal Constitution. Today, we are part of a great cultural and spiritual awakening that is heralding afresh the principles of liberty. Far larger than our own nation, this movement of freedom has both the promise and the vigor to signal the end of "man-as-god" totalitarianism in all of its forms the world over.

Together, as Americans, we must vow before Almighty God, the same solemn oath our revolutionary forebears proscribed nearly three centuries ago: that the rights of man come not from the hand of the state, but from the hand of God. And yet, we must acknowledge that the same foundational beliefs for which our forebears fought and to which we have sworn allegiance, are still at issue throughout our nation. Among our countrymen, the bedrock ideals of free enterprise, constitutional restraint and the repulse of statist controls are still in debate as our recent elections have borne out.

Yet, we dare not forget that we are heirs to the glorious legacy of Washington, and Jefferson. We must be highly resolved that the word shall go forth from our homes, our businesses and our communities, to both friends and antagonists alike, *that we the people* are unwilling to witness or permit the slow undoing of the work of liberty, to which this nation has always been committed, and to which it will always be committed. We cannot afford to yield to the discordant sound of statist ideals that appeal to our baser instincts of envy only to place us at odds and split our land asunder with class warfare.

Our freedom was not obtained through a stale trade document nor the approval of an international court! Rather it was born on the bloody greens of Lexington and Concord. A freedom to live, not a freedom to enslave. A freedom to strive, not a freedom from strife. We must pledge with one voice that as the work of liberty is advanced, the tyranny of King George shall not have passed away merely to be replaced by the far more iron tyranny of state enforced humanistic-utopian expectations.

This narrative exists as an engine to drive individuals, families, statesmen, churches and advocacy groups to push back the jungle of suspicion, discord, and moral decline in the realm of civil government. I am sounding the trumpet call to all concerned with the advance of liberty. This is a summons to join with us and to bear the burden of a long exacting struggle, year in and year out against the enslavement of intrusive government led by its countless minions of bureaucrats and their "fellow travelers" in the corporate world.

This fight for liberty will rarely be fought in the radiant light of the noon day sun, for freedom's zenith is not yet, nor will it be fought under the pale of utter darkness, for tyranny today lives in its last historic stand. Rather, it will be fought in the faint glow of freedom's dawn with the hope of ever increasing light. I refuse to believe that any of us would exchange places with any other people or any other generation. The nativistic urge to escape our current national and cultural challenges and exchange it for the illusion of an idyllic past way of life, must be as far from us as the east is from the west. Moreover it is the animating promise of the future that must guide our present course. Therefore, let the faith, the devotion, and the vision of liberty's expansion, light our path, and trust Almighty God that the glow from our fire will truly light the world. *Together we can undo the heavy burdens of bureaucratic government policies and loose the creativity, ingenuity and genius of the American people. Our commitment is without diminution and remains resolute. May this little book help you exhibit the same kind of energy, commitment and devotion as our forbears, so that we together, may see an expansion of the sphere wherein freedom's writ may run.*

CHAPTER ONE

The American Covenant Promise

He hath remembered his covenant forever, the word which he commanded to a thousand generations. Which covenant he made with Abraham, and his oath unto Isaac; And confirmed the same unto Jacob for a law, and to Israel for an everlasting covenant. Psalm 105:8-10

The overarching theme in Colonial-American life signaled an understanding that the sovereign God was creator of all things visible and invisible, and that He advances His rule throughout time and history by means of covenant. Meaning, that the God who created the universe, reveals himself in history, by laying down fixed-immutable ethical requirements, principles, and methodologies wherein His blessings may be known. To the colonial mind, God was distinct from His creation yet was continually intervening in the same. In relationship to these axioms, it was understood that God effects visible, concrete interactions, which include corporate and individual blessings; and negative sanctions relating to fidelity or infidelity to the same. Hence over time, early America held that God's covenant keeping people or "seed" is blessed and accrues a cultural dominion over all spheres of life, even while the "covenant breakers" are accursed, diminished, and eventually disinherited in national life. Ergo, from the first settlers to the Washingtonian founders, the notion of covenant was understood as the great pivot around which history revolves.

Now the basis for such understanding is found in Genesis 12:1-3, 13:16, 17:1-13 and 22:17-18. Herein the "Abrahamic Covenant" is depicted. Historically when you hear of the Scottish Presbyterians, English Puritans, or Augustinian Germans speak of 'The Covenant' they are invariably referring to the promises made to Abraham. Indeed, there is much within this narrative that is rich in "nation building" vision and principle. For promised to Abraham is greatness, honor, material wealth, personal increase, and a vital offspring, in order to bless and govern the nations according to God's precepts. It is instructive to note that God does not make the covenant with Abraham alone, but also with his children. This is significant for in turning our attention to the New Testament and Galatians 3:14-29, we find that through the finished work of Jesus Christ, all that are elect in God, The Church catholic, are now counted as Abraham's seed or children and are therefore heirs of the very same covenant promises and world changing mission as was given to the Hebrew commonwealth. Hence, to colonial America, a sacred trust had been passed on to their generation, and therefore the American Vision was an imperative, a divine mandate to build a righteous "city shining on a hill'. Ours was to be a new free nation that would herald liberty throughout the world and signal the overthrow of tyranny throughout the nations.

Moreover, according to the theme verses in Psalm 105, the Abrahamic Covenant is to be enforced and active for at least a thousand generations. Meaning there is still a long way to go before the full progress of the Church global and specifically the Church in America reaches its zenith. Practically speaking, Christians in America must re-anchor themselves in the worldview of their forefathers and then plan for the perpetuation of the Faith and for the greatness of The American Ideal for many generations to come. The sacred trust of the covenant must not only be passed to the next generation, but our children must be given the advantage of standing upon our shoulders and advancing the Faith, the vision of America, and of righteousness even further than we. That this futuristic vision runs in antithesis to the "mortgage the future" policies of President Obama cannot be understated.

But Isn't America A Secular State?

In fact "covenant thinking" and the primary doctrines of Christian Orthodoxy were once so pervasive and common in the embryonic stages of our nation that they were explicitly codified into colonial and state constitutions. As an example; the *Fundamental Constitutions of Carolina* forbade anyone from holding office or to own property that would not acknowledge the God of the Scriptures. In 1703, the Carolinas made it illegal for anyone to "deny any one of the persons of the Holy Trinity to be God," or to "deny the Christian religion to be true or the holy scriptures of both the Old and New Testament to be of divine authority." Similar declarations can be found in nearly all of the New England colonial and state charters as well as Virginia, Pennsylvania, New Jersey and Georgia. Beyond these codifications, the founders in their own words give eloquence to this covenant-nation motif. They still witness to the unique character our nation was to herald.

George Washington "Whereas it is the duty of all nations to acknowledge the providence of Almighty God, to obey His will, to be grateful for his benefits, and humbly to implore His protection and favor . . . . Now, therefore, I do recommend and assign Thursday, the twenty-sixth day of November next, to be devoted by the people of these United States . . . that we then may all unite unto him our sincere and humble thanks for His kind care and protection of the people of this country previous to their becoming a nation; for the signal and manifold mercies and the favorable interpositions of His providence in the course and conclusion of the late war; for the great degree of tranquility, union, and plenty which we have since enjoyed; for the peaceable and rational manner in which we have been enabled to establish constitutions of government for our safety and happiness, and particularly the national one now lately instituted; for the civil and religious liberty with which we are blessed . . . . And also that we may then unite in most humbly offering our prayers and supplications to the great Lord and Ruler of Nations, and beseech him to pardon our national and other transgressions . . . to promote the knowledge and practice of the true religion and virtue . . . . Given under my hand, at the city of New York, the 3rd of October, A.D. 1789"

Notice the covenant language of Washington's proclamation and its similitude to the aggregate passages we noted from Abraham's covenant promise in Genesis.

Patrick Henry "It cannot be emphasized too strongly or too often that this great nation was founded, not by religionists, but by Christians; not on religions, but on the Gospel of Jesus Christ. For this very reason peoples of other faiths have been afforded asylum, prosperity, and freedom of worship here."

On November 20, 1798, in his Last Will and Testament, Henry wrote: "This is all the inheritance I give to my dear family. The religion of Christ will give them one which will make them rich indeed."

Again in leaving an "inheritance" Henry exhibits covenantal thinking and the perpetuation of the vision!

John Hancock "RESOLVED, That it be, and hereby is recommended to the good People of this Colony of all Denominations, that THURSDAY the Eleventh Day of May next be set apart as a Day of Public Humiliation, Fasting and Prayer . . . to confess the sins . . . to implore the Forgiveness of all our Transgression . . . and a blessing on the Husbandry, Manufactures, and other lawful Employments of this People; and especially that the union of the American Colonies in Defense of their Rights (for hitherto we desire to thank Almighty GOD) may be preserved and confirmed . . . . And that AMERICA may soon behold a gracious Interposition of Heaven." By Order of the Massachusetts Provincial Congress, John Hancock, President.

See here the covenant thinking in terms of the relationship between ethics and economic prosperity!

Thomas Jefferson "God who gave us life gave us liberty. And can the liberties of a nation be thought secure when we have removed their only firm basis, a conviction in the minds of the people that these liberties are of the Gift of God? That they are not to be violated but with His wrath? Indeed, I tremble for my country when I reflect that God is just, that His justice cannot sleep forever.

"The democracy will cease to exist when you take away from those who are willing to work and give to those who would not . . . It is incumbent on every generation to pay its own debts as it goes. A principle which if acted on would save one-half the wars of the world . . . and I sincerely believe, with you, that banking establishments are more dangerous than standing armies; and that the principle of spending money to be paid by posterity, under the name of funding, is but swindling futurity on a large scale."

Now Jefferson is thought of as the essential founder of the Democratic Party. Pitted against Obama's bail-out culture of largesse, one must wonder if President Jefferson might resort to dueling pistols to regain his party's and nation's self-respect.

I can give many more such renderings from our embryonic beginnings, yet as late as 1983 The Democratically controlled US House of Representatives passed this incredible declaration!

"Whereas the Bible, the Word of God, has made a unique contribution in shaping the United States as a distinctive and blessed nation of people. Whereas Biblical teachings inspired concepts of civil government that are contained in our Declaration of Independence and the Constitution of The United States . . . Whereas that renewing

our knowledge of, and faith in God through Holy Scriptures can strengthen us as a nation and a people. Now therefore be it resolved . . . that the President is authorized and requested to designate 1983 as a national "Year of the Bible" in recognition of both the formative influence the Bible has been for our nation, and our national need to study and apply the teachings of the Holy Scriptures."

February 3, 1983—President Ronald Reagan issued the above requested proclamation.

The Covenant Exists

The American Covenant exists whether men acknowledge such existence or not. Positively, its riches, provisions of mercy and grace, grand vision, and manifold blessings stand ready to propel America into a new strapping "Golden Age." Negatively it sanctions are like teeth which threaten to bite, sting, and bring us to ruination unless we turn from our perilous course of practical atheism. Recovering our heritage, thinking covenantaly, and finally acting on that "New World" covenant may very well determine the fate of the American Empire in THIS generation!

For we must consider that we shall be as a city upon a hill. The eyes of all people are upon us. So that if we shall deal falsely with our God in this work we have undertaken, and so cause Him to withdraw His present help from us, we shall be made a story and a by-word through the world. We shall open the mouths of enemies to speak evil of the ways of God, and all professors for God's sake. We shall shame the faces of many of God's worthy servants, and cause their prayers to be turned into curses upon us till we be consumed out of the good land whither we are going. And to shut this discourse with that exhortation of Moses, that faithful servant of the Lord, in his last farewell to Israel, Deut. 30. "Beloved, there is now set before us life and death, good and evil," in that we are commanded this day to love the Lord our God, and to love one another, to walk in his ways and to keep his Commandments and his ordinance and his laws, and the articles of our Covenant with Him, that we may live and be multiplied, and that the Lord our God may bless us in the land whither we go to possess it. But if our hearts shall turn away, so that we will not obey, but shall be seduced, and worship other Gods, our pleasure and profits, and serve them; it is propounded unto us this day, we shall surely perish out of the good land whither we pass over this vast sea to possess it. Therefore let us choose life, that we and our seed may live, by obeying His voice and cleaving to Him, for He is our life and our prosperity."

JOHN WINTHROP

CHAPTER TWO

Vision and Purposeful Wealth

In the early morning light of the 21st century, American business culture evidences an insidious infection marked by the symptoms of a fuzzy relational and communal malaise. This weepy sentimentality has dispossessed the will to win, a desire to beat the competition, and to emerge singularly victorious in commerce. Such relationalism values a second-rate socialistic business ethic over and against the rambunctious spirit of enterprise, competition, and intoxicating ale of triumph once common in our great nation. In essence, Sesame Street has usurped Wall Street and there are no winners or losers just the marvelous mediocrity of the mushy middle. Hence a reliance on Federal power, interventions, bail-outs and a host of other blunt force tyrannical instruments have become the vogue not only among government elites, but also the executive class.

I recall a consultation with one of my customers. At the time we were engaged in the development of an aggressive marketing plan that would propel his business to far greater visibility. Inherent in the plan was the defeat of one of his chief competitors whose product line while similar was nevertheless inferior. My client was appalled that I actually spoke in terms of defeating his competition. "He has a right to work too!" he exclaimed. I responded that his competitors right to work was not at issue, it was whether or not my client felt it was his responsibility to guarantee his rivals success. My man certainly wanted to win, but not completely. He wanted to prosper, but not too much. He had a vision for expansion, but not if it meant the vanquishing of lesser opponents. Such double-mindedness is the Keynesian primordial ooze from which Obamanation has spawned

Now, in the midst of recession, is the time to redefine our current business environs in a more traditional light. A world of winning and losing, of struggle and vigor, and the hope of prosperity and greater personal freedom. Decisively, this generation has a cardinal opportunity to envision a new golden era of strapping American enterprise, to rebuff defeatist ideals, and replace them with time proven principles that will reinvigorate a business world-view of victory! *After all "You can't beat something with nothing."*

Worldview

The importance of having a fully articulated world-life-view is paramount in any successful business venture. By worldview I mean a set of beliefs and presuppositions that govern your sense of reality or how things work in time and history. It's never a question of worldview or no worldview, but only a question of whose worldview has gained the ascendancy in your life or vocation. Fascists, Communists, and Socialists have a worldview. Christians, Muslims, and Hindus have a worldview. Environmentalists have a worldview and capitalists have a worldview. Children have a worldview that is dramatically at odds with the worldview of adults. The concept itself is inescapable.

Most people are something of a composite of various views. Subconsciously they attempt to harmonize these sometimes desperate elements into something unique for them. The common refrain "It works for me . . ." has a certain merit. Unfortunately, such amalgams rarely work long term in that the smorgasbord of ideas that form an immature world-life-view are often in contradiction. Some like this "dynamic tension" and tend to ride their own shockwave enjoying a time of success until the inevitable breakdown takes place. It is precisely at the time of breakdown that unhealthy and non-productive notions often enter into the life of an entrepreneur or the management of given corporation. In other words without a well thought out sense of reality, of values, and of your place in the business world, your life may be easily hijacked to places you never intended to go. Remember, if you are not conscious of any particular worldview governing your life, someone, some institution, or some circumstance will cheerfully supply one for you. The question then will be whether or not such views find you successful in the marketplace or utterly miserable, lost, and groping for the reasons why.

The American Way

The American economic miracle is a three-century exercise in applied worldview. There is no question that America has long been the world dominant standard for prosperity. To illustrate, while consulting with a member of the British Parliament, it was remarked to me in a rather nonchalant manner, that Europeans are rich, but Americans are that much richer. This is true not only in terms of the sheer size of our economy, but the vast array of economic choices that are available to us. The question remains why are these things so? Why has America prospered so much and for so long even when saddled by more modern innovations such as the "welfare state" and the ever greater encroachments of government regulation and burdensome taxation? The answer again revolves around worldview and the practical applications, ethics, traditions, and tactics, which are derived from the same.

We have all heard of the "Puritan work ethic." But what exactly does it mean? Is it simply a call to frugality and saving? Or was there something endemic to the embryonic American colonial period that helped shape a dynamic vision of prosperity? In other words what was the worldview that birthed the most prosperous and industrious people in the long history of the world?

The colonial period in America was a distinctly religious time. Christianity dominated New England and the basic worldview birthed by such convictions formed an economic ethos that exploded into unprecedented material prosperity and political freedom. The cornerstone of this worldview was a belief in the transcendent nature of God as the creator and governor of life. Under this belief system man created in God's image was handed the earth to dominate and to become productive. This productivity and "fruitfulness" was to then be utilized for the expansion of Christianity and its message. The colonial "Puritan" understood this creator-god to have given gifts, talents, opportunities, and spiritual blessings to each of the faithful in order achieve prosperous ends. At no time was the Divine seen as the direct dispenser of wealth. Each individual was responsible to use whatever talents they had to achieve as much they could for a greater end. Therefore the average colonial American saw striving for mastery and victory in commerce as a matter of eternal weight and significance. The ideals of excellence, craftsmanship, the accumulation of wealth, of leaving an inheritance and building a family legacy, of material and territorial expansion, all were generated by this religious fervor. Indeed, all of life was considered a gift from God, and man had the responsibility to preserve, develop, and rule the creation.

As consequence of this "divine imperative" to economic growth, a limited system of government in the form of the American Republic was developed that would safely guarantee the personal freedoms needed to enjoy private property, work, and productivity, and in the parlance of Jefferson; " . . . the pursuit of happiness." The greater manifestation of this world-life-view formed a sense of economic, cultural, and political destiny that engineered the great westward expansion of the United States and the conquest of the continent. This overarching sense of destiny gave birth in rapid succession to the great Industrial Revolution, the age of invention, and the spirit of competition that was best exemplified by that "force of nature" Teddy Roosevelt. Roosevelt believed that is was through strife and the readiness for strife that a man or a nation achieved greatness. His was not a view that heralded conflict for the sake of conflict, but instead a striving for mastery, for dominance, and yes, for greatness.

Now I can hear the cacophony of commercial pacifists with a long whining list of what I call "yeah buts." The "yeah buts" will get you every time! Their carping will always sound the alarm of abuse and malfeasance that are at times exhibited in free markets and in the rarified air of freedom. Yeah, but what about the monopolies, the robber barons, child labor, the "greed" of the 1980's or the more recent scandals with Enron or WorldCom? Nowhere have I suggested that the freedom to strive, to compete, or the desire for success and achievement in business is to be devoid of ethics! This is a subject that will be taken up more fully another time, but for now, suffice it to say that we are to battle with a sense of purpose, destiny and ethics that will not only see the accumulation of wealth but the enjoyment of the same with a good conscience.

Sphere of Influence

Few of us will be motivated by the idea of conquering a continent, as was the case with our forefathers. Yet, we all have a sphere of influence that takes into account geography, economics, relationships, and the role we are to play in shaping that micro-world. Do you look upon all you survey with a sense of destiny and leadership? If not, why not? And if not you, then who? Oh there will always be the armchair critic, the casual expert who will be all too glad to give you advice on why you won't be able to achieve. These defeatist fear-mongers may even come from within your own family. But what of that sense of destiny, that nagging desire to achieve, and the impulse to be the head and not the tail that burns deep within your heart? That inward sense of achievement must be fed, nurtured, and directed.

A strategic worldview of victory must be translated into tactical plans for commercial and personal success. In other words "what you view is what you do." If your world-life-view is one of doom and despair then you will accomplish little toward victorious results. But if you are intoxicated with a sense of destiny and a vision of expansion and prosperity, if you love the sting of battle and will not shirk from rigorous competition, if you wish to lead in your sphere of influence and to dominate the market place ethically, then you have laid the foundation for success and satisfaction. In fact you've decided to become a "John Wayne" while eschewing "John Whine."

Having a fully articulated world-life-view is the key element in defining the battlefields of life. That is to be the one that *establishes the rules of the game*, who takes the initiative and makes the "other guy" respond to you! In political life, the paranoid candidate is always concerned about "opposition research." Such insecure creatures are only assuaged when they think they have all of the appropriate responses to whatever their rival might do or say. For such, the idea of fielding their own agenda and even ignoring the opposition's lesser ideas is somewhat foreign. Yet, the true statesman always stakes out the philosophical high ground and makes his opponents respond to his initiatives. The same principle is true in business and in all of life.

To possess battlefield awareness is to understand your reasons for entering into the arena of commerce. Surely, you want to prosper but to what end? What is your intention and objective? Once you have this understanding, prosperity has purpose and becomes the power to achieve the greater end. This pursuit is in no way a pacifistic endeavor. There will be obstacles, mind-numbing fatigue, seemingly indefatigable foes, and at times a sense of being overwhelmed. It is during these trials that the understanding of the purpose of your mission may very well be your only solace.

Prosperity is the power behind hopes and aspirations. It is a means to an end and not an end in and of itself. Once you see this you have a proper comprehension of the battlefield of business and commerce. What you will have developed is a core world-life-view of victory that will govern and animate all of your endeavors. Without such purpose you will be adrift and aimless, susceptible to the siren song of mediocrity. You literally *can't afford* such anthems governing your life!

Charge!

Once, you understand your environs and have developed a world-life-view to dominate the same you are by default in leadership. "He who reads leads . . ." is an axiom that bears weight and significance. Yet, whether your personal character, fortitude, and courage can actually demonstrate what you know to be true is another issue altogether.

Leadership is a quality much admired in political and business ranks. Unfortunately, leadership is also quite lacking in today's commercial environs and most especially in American political life. Much of this is due to the lack of the aforementioned "proper worldview."

All leadership is driven by vision! It is the engine from which all other aspects related to success are advanced. Yet leadership is more than having a great idea or lofty dream. Leadership must be demonstrated by the courage to act, and maintained by an indefatigable will. These are the essential elements for effective statesmanship or commerce. Vision does not occur in a vacuum! It requires reading and development! This is far more than trendy periodicals, opinion polls, or the latest "Power Point" innovation from some faceless MBA! True enlightened leadership requires the reading of the greater works of philosophy, history, theology, science and that most neglected of documents, The Federal Constitution. In all, these will all act as a furnace to forge great thoughts, great ideas, and a mental acuity that is able to seize the day!

Moreover, effective leadership is able to translate strategic thoughts to tactical plans In a political context, ideology must be married to practical solutions. Add to this rhetoric, personal inspiration of your political base and an unquenchable work ethic and you have the right ingredients that will make others respond to you and your initiatives.

Now we come to that essential element of leadership without which nothing can be accomplished. Courage! Granted courage without knowledge is the realm of fools! Yet, knowledge uncoupled to courage has little value. Teddy Roosevelt penned 35 books and was the winner of The Nobel Peace Prize. His intellect was keen. But, it was that singular act of courage in the charge of San Juan Hill that created the platform from which his knowledge could best be employed.

Further, it takes many acts of courage to lead up to that "San Juan" experience. With TR, many personal challenges, heartaches, and confrontations were faced head-on, long before he led the Roughriders. This character development is evidenced in the deportment and stature of the statesman or executive. Courage becomes a dignified garment more than any singular act. Hence, a true leader is able to command the field, more by what he is, than what he says.

A courageous character is not built through confession anymore than standing in a garage makes one an automobile. The assails of life, the challenge of life, the strengthening of the heart through trial, and conflict, all these take our measure and cause our growth.

End Game

Worldview, knowledge, strategic thought and the courage to act, taken together are the minimal requirements for success in business or statesmanship.

Let's face it; most of our societal interactions are hampered by minimalist expectations. How many executives know the difference between the economic theories of John Maynard Keynes and Ludwig Von Mises? Have they read the Communist Manifesto? Have they ever heard of the "New Deal" or "The Great Society" let alone understand the combined deleterious effects these programs have had on economic progress? Do they have an understanding of unalienable rights as depicted in the bill of rights? No, these are not questions for the intellectual "elite" and in fact, are basic ideas, which even the marvelously mediocre of our culture once knew! Leadership can and must take the field and fill the vacuum created by our societal lack of knowledge. Without these principles the modern grey flannelled management minion is left to beat the air.

The executive, professional, or statesman that develops a worldview and philosophy of prosperity and cultivates courageous leadership to act upon the same, to him belong the spoils that only victory can bring. Herein is a foundation we can rely on for generations and not the hollow mantra of change Obama style.

CHAPTER THREE

Worldview Impact

The notion of possessing a world-life-view is an inescapable concept of life. Even a child, though not epistemologically self-aware, still holds to a particular worldview. In other words, it his way of organizing facts, experiences, and impressions into a life system, wherein he will define his reality, his basis of truth, and thus take corresponding action. Such experiences and actions will be primitive and very limited, lacking mature experience and context, but never-the-less form a worldview.

Ergo, it is never a question of having a worldview or not having worldview. It is instead a question of what or whose worldview is in ascendancy. Nor is it a question of sophistication or understanding. Worldviews exist with or without a conscious cogent, articulation of the same.

In a larger context, Marxists have a worldview and Fascists have a worldview. So too Christians and Muslims, Western linear historical thinkers and Eastern circular realists, as well as conspiratorialists and rationalists all these have a worldview. That these views continually battle for supremacy are of utmost importance in defining how we relate to government, the notion of individual rights, and the definition of who we are and where we are going.

Worldview: The State and Individual "Rights"

To a man, our Founding Fathers rightly held that the "rights" of man come not from the generosity of the state but from the hand of God. Organically a "right" is an area to which no authority may speak and which no authority may invade.

On the other hand, totalitarians, statists and other "man as god" regimes hold that there is no area exempt from state authority. These all, with one voice see that there is no place for individuals; and that nothing exists outside of the state, since for them, the highest end of man is the State.

Yet clearly, God while granting certain unalienable rights to individuals also established the state. The state serves to bring a social cohesion and identification; it serves as an administrator of justice, and provides for a common defense.

Without a transcendent authority providing both individual rights, and laws of governance replete with proper jurisdictional authority, freedom as conceived by our forbears cannot long endure. Governance is more than state power, but includes basic self control, family governance, religious allegiances, commercial ethics and then finally political structures. Our Founders looked to the political as the governance of last resort. There was no concept of interventions into the other spheres of authority except to redress criminal actions.

The Declaration of Independence's spinal cord of thought "God-the creator who endows" stands in sharp relief to the modernists' concept of state power. Herein is the presupposition of a transcendent God perfectly ordered, yet at the same time, immanently revealed in history through the individual rights and principles as described in the document. Therefore the new political nation and individuality are held equally yet jurisdictionally defined by God. Therefore, neither the state, nor individuality may be exalted over the other. Both are under Divine authority.

John Locke vs. Barack Obama

While our founders were of course influenced by a Western and orthodox Christian culture, there existed more than a few political and social theorists that made, what were then, unprecedented applications of theistic philosophy to political social theory. Chief among them was John Locke. Locke held that men derived their rights from God, but voluntarily consented to give up a portion of them to institute governments for and limited to the protecting of life, liberty, and property.

Locke then proposed a social contract, because he saw that men were not perfect (an acknowledgement of sin nature) and thus would not uphold the rights of others in a non-governmental state of being. Therefore, men consent together to form a society to govern the state of sinful men, for self-preservation and those things seen as necessary to that preservation or life, liberty, and property. This governance was based upon the "consent of the governed" and the ability of "reasonable men" to discern just laws. *The end purpose of the government was to preserve life, liberty, and property.* If a ruler or ruling body, broke that contract by oppressing individual rights again pertaining to life, liberty and property, the people had not only the right, but an obligation before God to overthrow that same governance.

The election of Barack Obama points to a dominate worldview at odds with that of Locke and the founders. This utopian motif deems mankind as essentially good but whose ultimate evolution and realization can only be found in a political state of unity. The political end of governance coercively suppresses individual "rights" in exchange for a collective security wherein the political entity is not the last resort, but is the beginning and the end of every iota of life.

Conclusion

The worldview of our Founding Fathers birthed the freest, most prosperous, and life affirming nation the world has yet know. A worldview that sees the Creator-God endowing men with unalienable rights. These rights cannot be taken away. President Obama's election points to a state wherein the government as god determines who is free, who lives, who dies, and defines our existence from cradle to grave. Rights can be dispensed or taken away by Federal edict. The choice for you dear reader is simple. What kind of America do you want to live in? Who is your God? The Founders demand your reply!

Benjamin Franklin: "God governs in the affairs of man. And if a sparrow cannot fall to the ground without his notice, is it probable that an empire can rise without His aid? We have been assured in the Sacred Writings that except the Lord build the house, they labor in vain that build it. I firmly believe this. I also believe that, without His concurring aid, we shall succeed in this political building no better than the builders of Babel"—*Constitutional Convention of 1787 | original manuscript of this speech*

Thomas Jefferson: "God who gave us life gave us liberty. And can the liberties of a nation be thought secure when we have removed their only firm basis, a conviction in the minds of the people that these liberties are a gift from God? That they are not to be violated but with His wrath? Indeed I tremble for my country when I reflect that God is just, and that His justice cannot sleep forever." (excerpts are inscribed on the walls of the Jefferson Memorial in the nations capital) [Source: Merrill D. Peterson, ed., Jefferson Writings, (New York: Literary Classics of the United States, Inc., 1984), Vol. IV, p. 289. From Jefferson's Notes on the State of Virginia, Query XVIII, 1781.]

John Adams: "Each individual of the society has a right to be protected by it in the enjoyment of his life, liberty, and property, according to standing laws. He is obliged, consequently, to contribute his share to the expense of this protection; and to give his personal service, or an equivalent, when necessary. But no part of the property of any individual can, with justice, be taken from him, or applied to public uses, without his own consent, or that of the representative body of the people. In fine, the people of this commonwealth are not controllable by any other laws than those to which their constitutional representative body have given their consent."

CHAPTER FOUR

Christian American Patriot Vision

Should the Christian patriot be involved in political activity? Is there a legitimate issue in the separation of church and state that would inhibit such endeavors? And shouldn't Christians, as some would assert, simply take care of their own lives and leave everyone else alone?

Unswervingly, Christians are called to be dynamically active, not only politically, but in all spheres of life. Christians are not to live a life of self-centered introspection, but of service. Such service would include involvement in the various strata of civil government. Christianity does not depend on political means for the success of its mission, yet, involvement in civil government is meaningful, for it is one of the divinely chartered institutions of social order. The other governing institutions signified by self-government, the role of the family, and the Church.

The operative word here is Christianity, which is a far larger nomenclature than any one church structure or denomination. In other words, the Christian patriot is to act in spreading the good news of Christ's Gospel along with the moral instruction of God's Word into the political realm. This in no way suggests an organizational takeover of the state by the church, nor that the church neglect her ecclesiastical duties. Simply put, Christians are to be salt and light in the arena of politics, as in any other realm. Whereas the visible, institutional Church is to function in her Levitical and Prophetic role, instructing the civil magistrate as to the duties and requirements of God's law, and when needs must, rebuking the same, when God's Law is impugned or ignored.

The goal of Christian activity in the political sphere is not a dictatorial theocracy, but the support of a decentralized republic that acknowledges Christ as Lord. A true Christian patriot will not place significance on political coercion, for the state is not God, nor should it be viewed as the great moral engine to mold human ethical behavior. The proper stimulus for involvement in the civil realm is to render politics much weaker, for the state has taken on a monolithic, messianic character that has suppressed ecclesiastical, familial, and self-government. Practically, this translates into aspiration and work for smaller civil government, less taxation, and more individual freedom. The Scriptures do not favor an ecclesiastical elite, or a specific church body, ruling over the populace, nor are Christians to have hope in political salvation. In fact, our Puritan and Pilgrim forefathers arrived on these shores fleeing such religious tyranny.

The Christian patriot should abhor the idea of the state imposition of religious polity and doctrine, in other words the state controlling the church. A smaller civil government would be less tempted to violate the establishment clause of the First Amendment. Presently, our Federal government through the auspices of the IRS, has established what it considers a "legitimate church" through the creation of the 501c3 tax-exempt status. This is a clear attempt to establish a state religion and control the Church. Accordingly, such regulation is blatantly unconstitutional. Christian patriots must resist all efforts to undermine or eviscerate a biblical understanding of the First Amendment of the Constitution. The ACLU has not, does not, and must not be allowed to define the purpose and scope of this amendment.

Hence, the Christian patriot must see that both the church and the state, are established by God as separate institutions, that are not to undermine, nor interfere with each others respective duties. To the Church is given the "power of the keys" to bind into fellowship and instruct its members, and when necessary sanction and excommunicate the unrepentant. The state is given the "power of the sword" to promote and reward righteousness, and to punish and restrain wickedness. Accordingly, the Church and the state in juxtaposition, are to be viewed as augmentations one to the other, in the honoring of Christ and His Crown.

Therefore, Christians are not prohibited from involvement in the civic sphere, nor is the Church to be silent in her moral directives to the state. The state must uphold the law of God thus promoting maximum liberty and justice for all. The state is to protect the Church, so that she is free to perform her divine charter. The Church must educate the state regarding its understanding of God's Law and how it is to be applied.

Finally, it is imperative that Christian patriot realize that all of life (including politics) is religious. It is never a question of religion or no religion only a question of whose religion. Thus, one must acknowledge the impossibility of divorcing religion from the civil sphere. Civil government will reflect the notions and ideas of the dominate religion of that day. For example; the religion of Secular Humanism supports the "freedom" to practice pornography, abortion, and euthanasia. Economically, Humanism supports forced socialistic-wealth-redistribution and the welfare state. It's idea of law punishes the victims of crime and seeks to excuse lawless behavior. Some see this as the ultimate in political freedom, yet, the religion of secularism in application, abuses women, robs the unborn and the elderly of life and liberty, restricts or confiscates private property, and creates conditions wherein lawless behavior threatens moral anarchy and social collapse. In contrast to secularism, Christianity displays the kindness, benevolence, liberty, law and justice that established and prospered America for over 200 years.

Consequently, the Christian patriot, while supporting the separation of church and state, must understand that neither institution is separate from God. Finally, only a Christian ethic, undergirded by an explicit confession of Christ's lordship in our founding documents is able to support a truly decentralized constitutional republic. Only in this context, can notions of life, liberty under God, and the blessings of prosperity be fully realized. A goal that every true patriot must be willing to pledge their lives, riches, and sacred honor to promote and defend.

CHAPTER FIVE

The Creedal Basis of Free Enterprise

With the presidency Barak Obama upon us, we will undoubtedly hear a constant diet of grandiose swelling rhetoric concerning a myriad of salvific interventions of the Federal government into our current economic malaise. Many will embrace such "salvation" even at the expense of their own liberty. This devolution of thought is akin to a vertebrate metamorphosing into a jellyfish.

Yet as late as John F. Kennedy's 1960 inaugural address wherein he stated that " . . . the rights of man come not from the generosity of the state but from the hand of God" the concept of Christian Orthodoxy as foundational to human freedom was an assumed pinion of Western political thought. This notion is antithetical to the Obamanation motif which heralds the nihilistic homosexual John Keynes as a benign engine leading to Karl Marx as the ideal. The order which Kennedy acknowledged had many adherents. Yet its' most ardent apologetic came from French economist Fredrick Bastiat who wrote his missive "The Law" in response to godless economic tyranny.

In examining Fredrick Bastiat's economic theories (IE: Reagan Revolution) his theocentric worldview is an assumed fact of free markets. Yet what was once common knowledge is not so common today. Therefore, if we are to understand the economic theory of Fredrick Bastiat we have to understand his "creedal presuppositions." For this discussion I will briefly outline these axioms using the familiar Nicene Creed.

The Nicene Creed

I believe in one God, the Father Almighty, Maker of heaven and earth and of all things visible and invisible.

And in one Lord Jesus Christ, the only-begotten Son of God, begotten of His Father before all worlds, God of God, Light of Light, Very God of Very God, Begotten, not made, Being of one substance with the Father, By whom all things were made; Who for us men and for our salvation came down from heaven And was incarnate by the Holy Ghost of the Virgin Mary And was made man; And as crucified under Pontius Pilate. He suffered and was buried; And the third day He rose again according to the Scriptures; And ascended into heaven, And sitteth on the right of the Father; And he shall come again with glory to judge both the quick and the dead; Whose kingdom shall have no end.

And I believe in the Holy Ghost, The Lord and Giver of Life, Who proceedeth from the Father and the Son, Who with the Father and the Son together is worshiped and glorified, Who spake by the Prophets. And I believe one holy Christian and Apostolic Church. I acknowledge one Baptism for the remission of sins, And I look for the resurrection of the dead; and the life of the world to come. Amen.

As depicted in the First Article of the creed, God's transcendent nature is conclusively rendered. Meaning that God is the sovereign creator who established all things both visible and invisible and who is distinct and apart from his creation. Genesis 1:1, Colossians 1:16,17. Hence, the God who created you is the Lord and the giver of life. It is God who sustains your body, your soul, your senses, your reasoning faculties. It is God who provides your sustenance, your house and home, your family and property. It is God who nurtures you and protects you from all evil. He does all of these things expressly for his divine pleasure and purpose. As the creature you stand in God's image with a plenipotentiary role and divinely secured rights to increase and prosper.

Some of the basic concepts of liberty and freedom derived from the first article of Nicene or the notion of the transcendent—creator—God are as follows:

1) The *right to life* is a freedom granted by God. It is the transcendent-creator God who alone gives life. Any unlawful taking of life is murder. Therefore, if state sanctioned, state sponsored murder in the form of abortion is

codified, you have a denial of God's transcendence and have become tyranny to the unborn. Yet, this abomination is done under the aegis of a kind of humanistic "liberty" with rhetoric that is "pro-choice." This so-called "liberty" is deity-denying and thus ends in the persecution and the death of the unborn. Beyond the immediacy of the horrid deed itself, such tyranny leads to the destruction of whole generations and thus a culture of death is perpetuated until that nation or culture is annihilated. Consequently, unless liberty under God is recognized, tyranny and death are the results not only for the unborn, but eventually, for the elderly, the sick, the infirmed and finally society as a whole.

2) The second major principle of liberty derived from the first article is that provision, and thus *personal property* comes from God and God alone. The same God that created the earth gave man dominion over it. *Genesis 1:26-28* depicts man possessing ruling, and reordering the earth. Also, throughout God's Law, the possession of land is a mark of God's blessing and provision. Therefore, your family, your home, your property is a freedom and blessing that comes from God and not the state!

Ergo, all Fabian socialists, Marxists, Fascists and any other collectivist-statist ideals (Clinton) are attempts to usurp God and constitute a direct assault against personal property. How? If the state through coercive-abusive taxation, wealth redistribution or other paternalistic collectivist notions becomes your provider, in which you "live and move and have your being," what right do you have to personal property? Who is your God? If the state gives, the state can take away, blessed be the name of the state. The denial of the truths expounded in the first article of the Nicene Creed is a denial of God's transcendence and thus is a denial of the divinely secured freedoms of *"life, liberty and property."*

The second article of the Nicene Creed establishes Christ as both fully god and fully man yet diminished in neither aspect. Meaning, Christ's authority and rule is not confined to the spiritual or the unseen, but also extends to the visible-material world. For this reason, Christ's Lordship is comprehensive in scope and absolute in power. In an individual salvific sense, we see it is Christ who has secured our redemption. Signifying, the elect have been made free from the power of sin, liberated from eternal damnation and freed from the curse of the law. (Galatians 3:13) So too, the redeemed have been delivered from the power of this present world system, liberated from bondage to Satan and the dominion of sin, and freed from the sting of death. (I Corinthians 15:55-57) Finally, the elect have been redeemed as Kings and Priests to testify of Christ's dominion in the earth. (Revelation 1:6)

With the second article of the Nicene Creed as a foundation, we in alliance with Bastiat can make the following deductions in regard to liberty.

1) Christ is fully god and fully man diminished in neither aspect. Which means His lordship and His plenipotentiary (governmental) authority is exhaustive. In other words, Christ's rule is not confined to the invisible, for Jesus was incarnate into the visible-material world and so His rule extends to all spheres of life. This includes but is not limited to church life, family Life, economic life, and political life. Only in this context can notions of liberty thrive. Without the Crown and Covenant of Christ acknowledged, pluralism (many moralities) leads to the disintegration of society. It is instructive to note that tyrants tend to recruit religious pietists whose world-life-view confines the rule of Christ to the unseen or the spiritual (monasticism). In this context, the church would not resist the tyrant nor confront the tyrant with the claims of Christ, for the pietist denies Christ's Crown and Covenant in the material world. Their belief holds that Christianity has nothing at all to say regarding civil polity or any other societal discipline. This notion has been contested with vigor by Pope Benedict in his landmark book "The Spirit of the Liturgy".

2) As Christ saves and justifies the elect, they are saved from sin and delivered from religious coercion. The Reformation and recently Popes John Paul II and Benedict have signaled the end of political tyranny, for men have come to understand that it is God alone who justifies through the finished work of Christ and not the state nor any other institution. This emancipating ideal was not welcomed by those who wished the continuation of the slavish and feudal-political-economic paradigm of medieval Europe, nor is justification by faith and its resultant force toward freedom (Galatians 5:1) appreciated by statist collectivist tyrants today in whatever guise they don.

The third article of the Nicene Creed establishes one *Holy Christian and Apostolic Church*. The Church is the embassy of God on earth which represents his kingdom and rule through her Levitical (instructional) and Prophetic role. The Church is institutionally separate from the state. It must be free from all statist coercion to fulfill the Great Commission, which is to teach and bring under subjection through conversion all the nations of the earth to the claims of Christ. In the words of Cornelius Van Til " . . . the Biblical ideal or the sum of God's will is the transformation of the world, every part of it, into a place of worship for Christ." The Church under God is the primary engine for this global task of emancipation.

Principles of liberty derived from the third article of Nicea.

1) The Church is under God. The state is under God. Both, must acknowledge God and perform their respective duties according to His law. The Church is to instruct and when necessary rebuke the civil magistrate as to the ways of Christ. The state under God must punish lawbreakers and protect the church so that she is free to perform her divine charter. The Church and the state are not institutionally mingled. They are separate from each other but are not separate from God.

2) The Church has been given all the divine means to accomplish the Great Commission. The finished work of Christ, the Word of God, the sacraments, and the Holy Spirit proceeding from the Father will bring all things under the subjection of Christ. Thus, the notion of Gospel liberty being shed throughout the world is divinely guaranteed to succeed. The enemies of liberty have throughout history resisted and persecuted the Church, systematically seeking to silence her Levitical and Prophetic voice. The Church as God's embassy has been the bulwark to bring justice, righteousness and liberty to the nations. She cannot and will not be defeated by the tyranny of man.

Humanism, Liberalism and Christian Orthodoxy

Humanism, replete with its own manifesto is a full orbed religion that aspires to the deification of man through statist, pagan and occultic influences. In repudiating Christian orthodoxy, principally the notion of God's transcendence, Humanism becomes an amply articulated antichristian worldview. The humanistic notion of freedom elevates the state to the place of God and positions it as the author and protector of liberty. Thus from beginning to end, man is to be dependent on the state.

In operation, the kingdom of Humanism has touched every social institution in our nation including the Church. The power of Humanism practically applied could be termed "liberalism." When found in the Church, liberalism attacks the orthodox ideal so as to reinterpret God in man's image. In civil polity, liberalism becomes an imperialistic collectivist juggernaut that endeavors to knit all societal structures including the family and church, under its domain. We see this humanistic-collectivist belief principally in Genesis 13:1-9 with the building of the tower of Babel.

The world-life-view of Humanism can be depicted as a scientific-intellectual elite who has through time, reinvented God and ethics in man's image; *the antithesis of the Biblical record.* Thus man as a kind of god engineers a "superior secular culture," ever evolving into a forced egalitarian cooperative society: theoretically resulting in the utopian ideal. In this context the progress of the state is akin to divinity itself and therefore any religion that would impede such progress, or would attempt to decentralize its power is regarded as retrograde, fit for marginalization and eventual eradication. This was the anthem of the French Revolution (which Bastiat repudiates) and all other utopian social-political movements.

In comparison, Humanism and Christian orthodoxy viewed as life systems, are in constant struggle and combat, the results of which have profound effects on liberty and freedom. Christian orthodoxy agrees with the nature of the Kingdom of God in that neutrality does not exist in any area of life. The primary notion being that all knowledge has its genesis and application in an orthodox worldview and that any other man-centered idea, philosophy, political social theory, economic models, educational theories, indeed man's civilization apart from the Western zenith, is at war with God. Therefore, the battle for liberty is between God's order and man's perceived autonomy or put another way between Christ and Caesar.

When autonomous man seeks liberty apart from God his tendency is first to revolution and anarchy. Hard on the heels of revolutionary chaos comes the political-social reordering of society, wherein anarchy is suppressed and messianic tyrannical statism is imposed (See Karl Marx and Das Capital). In such states virile expressions of the orthodox Faith are persecuted and the family becomes a factor of production. In other words true liberty is abandoned in favor of a secular religion and its resultant brutality. Could this happen in America? Has the process already begun?

Christian Orthodoxy and The American Experience

The primary doctrines of Christian Orthodoxy were once so pervasive and common in the embryonic stages of our nation that they were explicitly codified into colonial and state constitutions. As an example; the *Fundamental*

Constitutions of Carolina forbade anyone from holding office or to own property that would not acknowledge the God of the Scriptures. In 1703, the Carolinas made it illegal for anyone to "deny any one of the persons of the Holy Trinity to be God," or to "deny the Christian religion to be true or the holy scriptures of both the Old and New Testament to be of divine authority." Similar declarations can be found in nearly all of the New England colonial and state charters as well as Virginia, Pennsylvania, New Jersey and Georgia. The advantage of explicitly incorporating Christian Orthodoxy into civil polity is threefold.

1) Recognizing Christ's Crown and Covenant in the civil realm brings national divine blessing and advantage. Deuteronomy 4:1-8.

2) Explicitly tying God's law to civil procedural laws, guards against civil polity (IE: The Constitution) being pirated by corrupt alien worldviews as represented by the ACLU, Act-Up, Move-On, Barbara Streisand and the whole of bitter lesbians, environmentalist-earth—worshippers and effete old communist employees from the East German government.

3) Greater prosperity and progress may be enjoyed as life, liberty and property is protected even while evil is suppressed. Read: FREE ENTERPRISE.

Christian Orthodoxy as expressed in early American culture recognized that the transcendent-creator God had made all things both visible and invisible. Indeed, all life was considered a gift from God and that God gave man the responsibility to preserve, develop and rule the creation. God was seen granting regenerate man with faculties and gifts as well as earthly resources in order to achieve Godly prosperity. Biblical law was applied however imperfectly, to protect and prosper this mandate consequently promoting liberty and limiting tyranny.

It could be argued that early American Christians were so successful in uniting orthodoxy and culture, and so enjoyed the blessings of the resultant freedoms that they began to allow anti-orthodox notions in the back door.

As an example; while one can find many Christian notions expressed in the Declaration of Independence and the U.S. Constitution, the fact that no explicit mention of God and Christ can be found in them shows the deleterious effects of enlightenment rationalism, deism and humanism in muting the language. While it can be argued that The Constitution is simply procedural law, and that as long as a Christian cultural consensus exists, it will be used to promote Christian liberty, the fact that no acknowledgement exists to God brings a myriad of trouble, much of which is being acted out before our very eyes. For while a largely Christian culture did exist at the time of the Constitution's ratification, such a culture is no longer prevalent. Which means the Constitution and its "procedural law" is now more often than not applied with a pagan humanistic consensus.

The result is that our once assumed "liberties" are being systematically undermined and thrown down by those who would be tyranny through their messianic statist political agenda. Read: Change—Barak Obama.

Having laid down the foundations of orthodoxy we may now delve into Bastiat having his world-life-view. See the reference below. His missive while brief is still too long for this narrative. One last comment: Bastiat's little treatise "The Law" was stated to be the most influential over the "Gipper" President Ronald Reagan. Oh that a renascence of such prosperity may once again launch our nation into a golden era of strapping American power.

CHAPTER SIX

Resurrection Foundation

Throughout the realm of Western empires, and in the huts and villages of remote peoples groups throughout the world, the resurrection of Jesus Christ is annually hailed in festive Easter renewal, as it has been done for the last 2000 years. Yet, the true impact and comprehensiveness of this signal event, is little appreciated by those who should hold it in highest esteem, chiefly The Church of the living God.

Oh to be sure, each Easter season, as in all before it, feature the proper victorious liturgies, hymns, and homilies. These are all be trumpeted with proper fanfare. The message of forgiveness of sins in Christ, redemptive renewal, and of new beginnings is always heralded with vigor. Yet, few hear, and fewer live, the greatness of Christ's resurrection and its call upon our lives. For few understand that Christ not only died to redeem individuals from their sins, but also lives today, in an enthroned state, waiting for his adversaries to be made His footstool. And fewer still apprehend that the end goal of His enthronement and our redemption is the transformation of the world, every part of it, into a place of worship for Christ.

THEME PASSAGES

Ephesians 1:22-23, Matthew 28:18-20

Christ, who upholds all things by the word of his power, and the One by whom all things exist, demands by his very resurrection nature, the conformity of culture to His revealed will as contained in the Scriptures. Herein is the anthem depicted in both the narratives found in St. Paul's Epistle to Ephesus and St. Matthew's gospel epilogue commonly referred to as the "Great Commission."

To fully comprehend the reach of Christ's resurrection claims, it is useful to first define the notion of culture or *cultus*. Culture is defined as the sum result derived from the composition of action or expressions of adoration and worship. It is, by definition, an inherently religious term. Hence, all societal interactions, relationships, disciplines, structures, designs and so on, do in fact, reflect a locus of worship. Even if a totally secular, statist, man-centric motif is existent, the resultant culture will reflect that same absence of God. So the idea of culture as an expression of worship is an inescapable reality. In fact, it's never a question of god or no god, just a question of whose god has the cultural dominance. As a whole then, the biblical ideal heralds the conversion and transformation of culture according to the claims of Christ and His imperial resurrection order.

This optimistic view for the Christian, places its confidence in the superiority of the Gospel of a resurrected Christ and not the progress of man. Of course, there remains a recognition of the perversion of culture in all of its facets by the depravity of unregenerate man. Hence, in developing a Kingdom Culture, there is never an accommodation of evil in the world, but instead a supreme confidence in the power of God to reorder it.

DUALISM—CONFUSING JURISDICTION

The Resurrection message when properly apprehended sees Christ portrayed as the "transformer of culture" and therefore all dualistic thought must be abandoned! By dualism I mean the erroneous view that depicts the unseen world as inherently spiritual and the visible world as somehow evil. In other words the earth, the body, and material possessions are not evil in and of themselves. Therefore, we must expand our vision to see that Christ himself was incarnate into the physical world and was raised bodily, ergo extending his resurrection domain and jurisdiction into the physical world and never to be confined exclusively to the ethereal unseen!

So the material world is not creature and property of hellish design. Thus while one must acknowledge that sin and evil perverts the material world, one must equally understand that the Resurrected Christ and His Kingdom conquers and restores the same fallen world. *Therefore sin and evil is not the focal point and ground of theology, rather the true, holy, and living God is the ground upon which we stand.* Consequently, evil, sin and perversion do not in any way define the biblical end of theology. Satan is not in any sense king of the universe, neither in its material nor in it's spiritual aspect.

FEAR—DENIAL OF THE RESURECTION MESSAGE

Practically, Christians must abandon the fear of evil in the world in favor of the power and supremacy of the righteousness, and efficacious grace that is found in Christ. A Christocentric life is one that is filled with confidence in the future, and given to advancing the Kingdom with boldness in high and low places.

Fear of evil and even fear itself is the great weapon of Hell against the people of God. What Christ ordained as "The mighty "sons of thunder" become the whimpering hoards of irrelevancy, as the saints separate themselves from culture, fearful of its sinful attractions. The separatist cedes the ground to the very thing he fears, chiefly, evil. No such idea can be legitimately followed in light of the true message of a transformational understanding of the Ascended Christ!

Emphatically Christ is not against culture! Christ instead seeks to subjugate and reconstruct it through His reconciliatory work upon the cross. Christians then are not to grovel in dualistic, fatalistic bunkers of fear. Rather Christians, The Church, and with it the Kingdom of God are to advance, and press the claims of Christ, converting the culture to the worship the King of kings and Lord of lords. While the Kingdom of God begins inwardly through regeneration, it advances and is manifest without through our actions both individually and corporately. Finally, the Kingdom is to penetrate and predominate over the whole of our social existence

Given the greatness, expansiveness, and glory of the resurrected Christ, together with all its ramifications for the elect, we dare not hang our heads low in despair or despondency. Fear has no place in our vocabulary! All the vanities we are tempted with are eclipsed in the glory of His ascendancy! No obstacle, no challenge, no stronghold, indeed not even death itself, can invalidate the power of Christ demonstrated in His elect. When we act autonomously apart from this knowledge, we fall prey to the tempters snare of defeat and death! Now is the time to know Christ as He is and conform our actions to the fact of the resurrection!

GETTING IT RIGHT!

When we pray "thy kingdom come . . ." we are praying for the conversion of all aspects of man's existence to express the Glory of God. This worldview is supported by a conscience of righteousness in Christ, which basks in the knowledge that the saints have a forensic (judicial) "right standing" with God through Christ's finished work. This "right standing" leads to "right doing" and consequently, it is to be with unbounded confidence, hope, and faith that we are to conquer our fainthearted imperceptive vision. Such trepidation tramples the promise of the covenant ratified in His blood. We cannot allow such fears to rule the day lest we impugn all that Christ has secured on our behalf to make the world righteous in Him.

It is an oddity of history that the Church has little understood the greatness of Christ's resurrection claims, let alone acted upon them. Yet, dictators, kings, and despotic personalities have throughout time understood very well the social, political and cultural ramifications of THE KING OF KINGS. Their combined persecutions of the Church has sought to silence the embassy of God. Yet, in modern America, no such persecution is needed for the Church, for she has by her own ignorance and indolence, effectively placed a "reed" in the hand of Jesus, practically mocking his rightful kingship. Matthew 27:29-30.

May God grant us "eyes to see" Christ as He is! He's not a babe in a manger, nor is He a beaten visage on deaths tree, the cross. He is the resurrected Lord of Glory above princes, presidents, and all earthly pretenses of power. HE IS RISEN INDEED! For the sake of our Republic—ACT LIKE IT!

CHAPTER SEVEN

Of Faith, Fidelity, and Civil Witness

One of the many erroneous "Religious-Humanistic" charges against Orthodox expressions of The Christian Faith or vibrant demonstrations of Christian civil witness is that we care little or nothing at all for the doctrines and disciplines that theoretically lead to sanctification and holiness. In this context, the Religio-Humanist views Christianity as "private" and at its zenith "monastic" useful only for self-examination and otherworldliness. Such standards are valuable for the Religio-Humanist in that a self-imposed "ghettoization" for the Church is in harmony with their unintentional tyrannical vision of civil polity.

On the contrary, while transformational Christians, (those who hold that Christ's rule is not confined to the unseen world) hardily reject the monastic, introspective, legalistic and selfish "privatized religion" of these arrogant "will-worshiping" idolaters. (For the Religio-Humanist rejects Christ's cultural claims). We maintain with equal vigor and unbending determination our allegiance to Christ and the exhortation of both Old and New Testaments " . . . be ye holy as I am holy." Yet "holiness" and fidelity to the Biblical ideal, is not defined by those who walk in antithesis to Divine revelation. Hence, a true Christian should not define their existence nor judge themselves in accordance with a "man-centered paradigm" of holy living.

The differences between the Religio-Humanist and the true Christian concerning the question of holiness and fidelity revolves around two distinct areas of conflict.

FIRST The Source and Standard of Holiness

Christian orthodoxy holds, that God's grace is administered from Christ in His enthronement and is demonstrated by the Holy Spirit, consequently giving us the mercy, grace, and power to obey the revealed will of God as contained in the Scriptures. Herein is an objective, immutable standard that cannot be diluted by subjective, arbitrary man-based notions of "what ought to be". So as Christ has redeemed man by His meritorious work through crucifixion, so too He maintains and sanctifies His sons through His resurrected, ascended state by the power and efficacy of The Holy Spirit.

The Religio-Humanist believes that through monastic, legalistic, self-abasing acts of ritual to sully, mock and destroy the "flesh", the Church may be fully emancipated from the material world and escape any form of civil discourse. Their mantra maintains that the experience of the "inner light" or God infused into the essence man, can only be achieved through separation from the "world". The "God-infused" experience confines "holy" behavior to private subjective interpretations as the Religio-Humanist rejects any notion of Christ's authority in the visible world and culture. Hence man and his feelings are the final authority of ethics, and are not to be defined by Scriptures, nor authenticated by the Church. Consequently, the standard of holiness is man-centered, subjective, and capricious. It is never to be "seen" or demonstrated in the culture. It is the penultimate 'private' life.

SECOND The Scope of Holiness

Christianity contends that every person, family, every activity, relationship or human endeavor must be conformed to the Word of God and subsequently becomes the objective expression of "Holiness unto the Lord." This view of sanctification is applicable to the individual, the family, the Church and in civil affairs. The emphasis is comprehensive in scope. Individual sanctification leads to an outward witness that impacts the corporate Church and then society as a whole. Hence, the continual ongoing work of the maturation of The Church maintains that individual holiness is not independent of corporate holiness. True Christianity holds to a global vision of dominion through ethical reform. Ergo, there exist no false dichotomies between individual holiness and corporate expressions of the same. Such outward holy witness leads to the transformation of the world in every aspect. This is in keeping with the anthem of The Great Commission as described in St. Matthew chapter 28

The Religio-Humanist sees all spirituality in terms of the individual. They are ascetics who laboriously practice self-denial of physical and material pleasure or denial of civil concern in order to earn God's favor. Typically they eschew the institutional Church and wholly and altogether reject the notion of Christian Culture. They are separatists in terms of the "material and spiritual world" and create a false antithesis between a public vibrant Church acting as God's embassy and a private 'conscious' driven religion. Their end goal is the idea of man absorbed into divinity. For them the Church is an impediment, and the corporate Christian community a weight and encumbrance to their fictional quest of total, absolute, self-perfection.

Religio-Humanism—Unwitting Allies of Secularity

In the context of Secularized-Statist Humanism, we find a worldview that is replete with its own manifesto and is a full orbed statist-religion that aspires to the deification of man through totalitarian, pagan and occultic influences. In repudiating Christian orthodoxy, principally the notion of God's transcendence, Humanism becomes an amply articulated antichristian worldview. The humanistic notion of freedom elevates the state to the place of God and positions it as the author and protector of liberty. Thus from beginning to end, man is to be dependent on the state. Secular-Humanism can be depicted as a scientific-intellectual elite who has through time, reinvented God and ethics in man's image; *the antithesis of the Biblical record.* Thus man as a kind of "god" engineers an imagined "superior secular culture," ever evolving into a forced egalitarian cooperative society: theoretically resulting in the utopian ideal. In this context the progress of the state is akin to divinity itself and therefore any religion that would impede such progress, or would attempt to decentralize its power is regarded as retrograde, fit for marginalization and eventual eradication. To the Christian who holds Christ as the "transformer of culture" the anthem of Secular-Humanism signals an unyielding fight until one or the other is triumphant.

The Religio-Humanist is in full alliance with his secular brother. If not intellectually in league with such designs, certainly in point of fact, due to his social inaction and deliberate segregation of the ethical demands of Christ to the unseen. They are in the parlance of Joe Stalin "useful idiots" to the statist agenda. In fact they are often recruited by the statist to give legitimacy to the dictatorial motif, hence theoretically adverting opposition to the state.

The early Church was seen as a threat to the Roman Caesar-cult not due to a bulging militia, but because of its concern for true sanctification of social structures. As such they ethically and morally exposed the ethically rotted foundations of Imperial Rome. This pattern is repeated over and again whenever the Church's vitality is manifested in a particular culture or nation state. In colonial America, the clarion trumpet of the Church and the dynamic lives of her saints, became the fertile ground that led to our corporate revolt against the Crown of King George. The Church was also the first to be attacked by any of the 20th century examples of Marxist revolution. So a vital Church, rejecting the siren seductions of Religio-Humanism, will always lead in " . . . The transformation of the World, into a place of worship for Jesus Christ." In sum that is the chief end of "HOLINESS UNTO THE LORD".

Chapter Eight

Stop Whining!

I am not quite sure what the problem is: a renaissance of nihilistic thought, the corporate effects of new age Oprah Winfrey fads, a loss of historic perspective, a national dulling of the senses, or our own inbred Pollyanna denial of conflict, but America is infected with an unbalanced, unrealistic, and ultimately dangerous utopian view of national life. How is it that we so often ignore the vast historical data of our own national growth which depicts conflict, tumult, tribulation, pain, and suffering? A crucible which taken together with our own corporate Faith in God led to the building of the greatest nation yet known to man. Apparently socialistic ease is now esteemed over strife and competition leading to excellence and dominance. Witness the rise of Barack Obama. Fifty million plus American's voted for him so as to relieve their perceived stress. To which I say; "WHAT STRESS?" Compared to: Valley Forge? Gettysburg? Iwo Jima? Korea? Vietnam? The Cold War? Are we to esteem ease over freedom? If so, we deserve neither!

Scripturally The Apostle Paul makes more than a few references to the fighting's that are within and from without. Job the suffering servant, whose book is perhaps the oldest in Holy Writ, is also the least quoted in the modern world. Any gains of the Hebrew Commonwealth and the Kingdom of Israel were not without great sacrifice and upheaval. The Book of the Acts is replete with dramatic conversions, miracles, persecutions, martyrdom, political infighting, and intrigue. No evidence here of the peaceful mundane. The Master Himself said that "in this world, you will have tribulation." Such tribulation is not confined to physical persecution, imprisonment, or political tyranny. In fact, Scripture places far more weight and stress on our battles with sin, being sinned against, heartbreak, loss, and emotional hardship than it does outward oppression. The point here is that the people of God have always had conflict. Yet, Faith in God, the superiority of Christ over all that is contrary here, gave his people the holy "steel" for their corporate backbone to fulfill their divine destiny. A destiny which transcends and gives meaning to pain, suffering, and conflict.

In this light two principles beg to be considered for modern Americans.

1) Life does not revolve around you. Surprise! It was not too long ago that most people, both Christian and non-Christian, understood this salient fact. I'm quite sure that our grandparents, who knew the deprivations of the Great Depression, and the boys on Omaha Beach comprehended this certainty. However, our generation, driven by caprice and selfishness, along with a cult of victimization, seems to believe that every pleasure in life is "owed to them" and that all sorrow, disease, or calamity, should be kept far from them by some Federal intervention. To compound this problematic childishness, when the modern American does not get what he wants, he shifts blame for his every failure to a politico, religion, or even God. Such whining is reprehensible, but is still an obnoxious fact of the moderns. These actions are in the grand tradition of Adam's infamous reference to Eve in Genesis 3:12, wherein all blame is for his sin is shifted to the weaker vessel. Yet it is the "Adamic sin nature" that is remembered and not Eve. To paraphrase C.S. Lewis, life on planet Earth will never be so good, so as to forget the promise of heaven. It's time to grow up and reaffirm this truth.

2) Faith in a God-ordained national future is more than a confession. A cursory glance at Hebrews chapter 11 (the Hall of Fame of Faith) denotes not a litany of confessions, but instead a catalog of actions. As James declares, "faith without works is dead." It is too easy to complain and curse the darkness. No faith is required to recognize evil or chaff under its influence. But making a stand, as a real man, this requires faith. Faith is not comprised of false bravado brandished by those who boast in their prowess in a yet future "no-holds-barred" calamity (these are exceedingly rare). Faiths, and the acts of faith, are more generally played out in what might be termed "holy monotony." That is, doing your duty, in the church, the workplace, in the community, and for the nation with consistency and expectation, no matter how difficult or challenging it may be.

Staying the course without immediate reward or recompense was the great signal testimony of the "Father of Faith," even faithful Abraham. He saw the promise far off, yet, it was never fully realized in his lifetime. Such overarching vision guards the heart from selfishness, bitterness, and childish protest. Certainly, there is nothing profound in these principles. They were once a part and parcel of a very basic and rudimentary understanding of what it meant to be an American. Unfortunately, the longer I live, the more I realize just how great our cultural, social, and moral deprivation is. What was once basic has somehow become enigmatic. I'm reminded of a World War II ballad, "We are poor little lambs who have lost our way . . . baa baa black sheep."

Clearly, for the American Christian, such an immature testimony falls far below the royal pedigree that the Master has secured for us in His own blood. Therefore, we must highly resolve to turn the tide! We must strive for maturity, shame cowardice, expose the ignoble, agitate against the dishonorable, upbraid the unchivalrous, and put away childish things. That is, life on planet earth is at minimum difficult. *It stings!* Sometimes beyond imagination! Life is designed by God with a sharp edge so as to prepare us for greatness! Only the eyes of faith, undergirded by hope, can produce a sense of individual and national destiny, mature and fully functional, that will give honor to God and eclipse the wailing of victimization or the illusory hope of a pain-free existence without achievement.

POLITICAL FALLOUT

From a political perspective the utopian always rides the "back of the tiger" named envy. This has given rise to the cult of victimization leading to Communism, Fascism, and other statist designs. Unless the church first begins the eradication of such thoughts along with the accompanying fads, programs, and pandering, little will be done to rid the political culture of these insidious designs. It was Gen. Douglas MacArthur in his address to Congress who said; " . . . the political problems of our day are chiefly theological in nature. Only a spiritual revolution can blunt and tame man's passions." Indeed, in order for a new generation of Christian statesman to arise, pulpits and churchman alike will have to exchange the epistemology of the "belly" for the glory of Christ's Crown. Only then will true national renovation take place and America once the home of John Wayne, may silence forever the obnoxious cult of "John Whine."

CHAPTER NINE

Prayer That Matters!

There is a communion of men with God by which, having entered the heavenly sanctuary, appeal to him in person concerning his promises in order to experience, where necessity so demands, that what they believed was not vain, although he had promised it in word alone. John Calvin

This grand description of the legislative dynamic of prayer as taken from Calvin's introduction to the subject in his "Institutes of the Christian Religion," is an essential foundation for the Church to recover if she is to resolutely and effectively exercise her parliamentary role in the earth. Explicitly, this "communion of men" reach into the very seat of all governmental authority in heaven and earth through prayer. These prayers are marked not by sentimentality, mystical expression, nor monastic vain babbling. Rather from this lofty plane, they make appeal to the Father through Christ concerning divine legislation, chiefly, that which God has promised to perform in His Law-Word. As depicted, the Church, this "house of prayer for all nations" is asking the "God who keeps covenant forever" to execute his Word "where necessity so demands" thus advancing the Kingdom on "Earth as it is Heaven."

The aim here is not that the Church should pray for indeed she must even "without ceasing." Rather the stress is upon the legislative content of prayer. That is for the Church to rightly function in her governmental capacity, she must through prayer and public proclamation legislate God's will, as revealed alone in Scripture, on earth, thus enforcing the Crown Rights of Christ over all of life.

Again I must stress, that the body and form of these legislative-governing prayers are not subjective and cannot be formed by human instrumentality no matter how noble the thought may be. Rather such praying must be founded upon all that God has vouched to effect exclusively in the inspired and infallible Law-Word of God. God's written Word is peerless in that it alone is divinely guaranteed not to "return void" and to "accomplish that which I (God) please" even to "prosper in the thing whereto I (God) sent it."

Positive and Negative Sanctions

The promises of God could be defined as anything that God has vouched to perform. Specifically, the promises of Scripture are grouped throughout in covenantal structures. Within these structures, God promises blessings both spiritual and material for those, who, in the long term, obey His statutes. Through this inheritance of blessing, God multiplies and increases His covenant people, so that in turn, they may advance His purposes in the earth. Just as crucial to understand is that within the same covenantal structures, God promises negative sanctions both spiritual and material for those, who, in the long term, transgress and mock His Law. Thus through the covenantal curse, the wicked are disinherited in history. Through this dynamic of blessing and negative sanctions, the righteous accrue dominion in the earth.

As an example of the covenantal foundations of Scripture we examine the structure of Deuteronomy 28. The first verse exhorts the Israelite nation to hear, observe, and perform all the commandments which God had given for the expressed purpose of setting her high above all the nations of the earth. Then in the next 13 verses, all the blessings that were to be accrued in relation to their obedience are delineated. Literally blessings are conferred which are coextensive with all of life both spiritual and material and all given with the end of blessing the nations of the earth. However, in the 15th verse the transition to negative sanctions (curses) occurs. From this point until the end of the chapter, temporal but very real curses are delineated for long term disobedience and covenant breaking. Thus, the negative sanctions exist to disinherit, diminish and eventually destroy wicked unrepentant individuals and nations.

If then the church is to pray and make proclamation covenantally, she must embrace the statutes of Scripture, both the blessings and the curses. For both are inspired by God and necessary for the work of Divine governance.

King David At War

David the warrior king, was a man of covenant who approached civil polity and spiritual worship, with a firm understanding of positive and negative sanctions. Witness the first Psalm. David extols the virtues of the righteous man who delights in God's Law. He declares blessing and strength for the law-keeper. The righteous man is described as a tree planted by the water, which brings forth its fruit in due season, whose leaf does not wither. This man is shown to be prospering in "whatsoever he doeth".

However, David goes on to describe the lawbreaker as one who under the crushing weight of Divine wrath, becomes chaff driven by the wind, who cannot endure the judgment and will by virtue of his wickedness, perish from the earth. This covenantal understanding is paramount if we are to comprehend, embrace, and emulate David's imprecatory war Psalms and recapture our lawless society.

Let us examine the controversial 109th Psalm. David is at prayer warring against the enemies of God. In verses 4 and 5, David gives himself to prayer and describes his enemies as those who act with disdain for God and righteousness. From this forensic-legal ground he proceeds to proclaim and enforce the covenantal negative sanctions against these very same enemies in verses 6 through 29.
It is important to note that David is merely applying God's Law to specific conditions. That is each imprecation found in this Psalm is directly related to definite covenantal sanctions. *There is nothing of David here!*

All of his utterance is being inspired by God and applied to very real circumstances. Yet to the casual observer, the language is harsh even hateful. Indeed, this has caused great bewilderment for many learned men who have tried to reconcile such praying with the love ethic of Christ. C.S. Lewis for example found these Davidic imprecatory prayers so offensive that he ascribed them to demonic authorship. C.I. Scofield while not as brazen as Lewis, nevertheless asserts that the imprecatory Psalms amount to something of a Davidic temper tantrum, which under the "old dispensation" was excusable, yet in the "new" is less than desirable behavior.

While these views are common, they are also heretical and in the case of Lewis, blasphemous. Certainly these views (Lewis in particular), fail to take into account that God's Word is Divinely inspired, infallible, and immutable. Secondly, they fail to understand the covenantal continuity of both Old and New Testaments. What this means practically, is that unless the New Testament specifically changes, modifies, or nullifies an Old Testament principle, that principle is still in effect and is binding. Mr. Scofield and the adherents of dispensational thought find this proper covenantal hermeneutic somewhat disturbing in that it strips away the convoluted notions that the New Testament saint should never act "harsh and hateful" as David. However, David is not praying these prayers autonomously, but rather under Divine inspiration. Thus to assert that David is motivated by hate is to charge the God of Old and New Testaments with maniacal intentions.

Truly, many pietistic clergyman have maintained that the God of the Old Testament is full of wrath and hate and yet the very same God is full of sentiment and love in the New Testament. Rather than a Biblical depiction of the God who "is the same yesterday, today, and forever", their perception is of a truncated and schizophrenic deity who maintains an identity crises replete with subjective, mercurial and arbitrary actions. Due to these views, the pietistic, antinomian, dispensationalist framework denies any possibility of enforcing negative sanctions in the temporal yet inconsistently and hypocritically affirms Divine wrath in eternity. Such incongruent thinking is typical of anti-covenantalists.

The New Testament Speaks!

Another strange omission by these anemic evangelicals are the numerous imprecations which are found in the New Testament directly from the lips of Jesus and the apostles. For example, In Matthew 23 verses 13, 15, 16, 23, 24, 27, and 29, Christ unleashes a crushing cannonade upon the Pharisees in the form of a seven-fold curse upon their heads! Is this utterance inharmonious with the love of God? *Certainly not!* Rather this is a loving warning of the sure and swift negative sanctions that are about to fall upon those who have prostituted the Law of God if they do not repent. In fact Christ is delivering a covenantal lawsuit that will arrest their miscreant behavior either through repentance or horrific judgment.

Also, the apostle Paul declares anathema (eternal destruction) upon anyone "who loves not the Lord Jesus" in I Cor. 16:22. Again Paul grapples with heretics who were seeking to pervert the church at Galatia when he pronounces a curse upon them in Galatians 1:8 and again praying that they would be emasculated, neutered lest their heresy reproduce in chapter 5:12. In II Timothy 4:14 Paul invokes covenantal theology when he declares that Alexander the metal worker be repaid according to his deeds. Alexander resisted and caused great damage to Paul's ministry. *Question:*—Is this the same Paul who authored the great love chapter namely I Corinthians 13? Yes, indeed and the same God who moved upon him with Divine inspiration!

Real Churchmen Fight!

> For the weapons of our warfare are not carnal, but mighty through
> God to the pulling down of strongholds.
>
> —2 Corinthians 10:4

Our forefathers embraced covenantal imprecatory prayer as a potent and divine weapon that would demolish all opposition to the advance of the Kingdom of Christ. They were not a squeamish lot, and were fully prepared to prosecute the war against the lawless.

> We should pray that our enemies be converted and become our
> friends, and if not, that their doing and designing be bound to fail
> and have no success and that their persons perish rather than the
> Gospel and the Kingdom of Christ.
>
> —Martin Luther

> If any of the enemies of God's people belong to God's election, the
> Church's prayer against them giveth way to their conversion, and
> seeketh no more than that the judgment should follow them, only
> until they acknowledge their sin, turn, and seek God.
>
> —David Dickson

> That which is ridiculous deserves ridicule!
>
> —St. Augustine

Dear saints it is time to stand upon the covenants of Scripture. It is time to rise and strike for the advance of the Gospel. No shirkers nor cowards need apply. The call of Divine government is upon you. Will you be girded with terrible resolution as David? Will you join the "communion of men with God? Will you exercise dominion in al spheres of life? I pray so for the sake of your children and our Republic *SOLDIERS OF CHRIST ARISE.*

CHAPTER TEN

Play Ball!

The great dynasties of Major League Baseball have always maintained supremacy of the ball diamond through the development of supportive minor league teams more commonly referred to as the farm system. When properly supported, the farm team—minor league organization, cultivates young talent that can be employed for the "big leagues" when the need arises or the position has opened. This is an inherently "bottom-up" approach which in the long term provides a particular franchise with stability and success. While the age of "free agency" has modified this approach (using large sums of cash to buy a players contract), the farm-system comprised of home grown talent is still the dominant theme for long term stability and annual competiveness.

In the political world success is measured in the terms of victories, from which the projection of power determines policy. Even if one desires to decentralize and restrict political power, such polices must at some point be enacted from a position of authority. In order to achieve that influence one must field candidates, win races, and control political parties at the local level. Unfortunately, most politically active Christians think in terms that cripple any long term development of local "talent" which can then be called upon to cogently represent the claims of Christ in the "big leagues" of civil discourse and policy making.

In America, politically active Christians are eerily uniform in their reactive response to negative and sinful national trends. They are very good at the point of protest and can marshal grass roots outrage on the national stage. But as I oft declare "outrage" rarely wins battles! So even when Christians are victorious at blunting a particular onerous policy, such obsessions with all things national brings a woeful neglect to the gateways of political influence at the local level. Therefore we are always left to react to what the "bad guys" are doing instead of making them react to us. You can't play defense all the time and expect to take ground!

This negligence ensures that explicitly Christian thinking candidates are not developed. Hence; the saints are nearly always left outside the political process, first at the local level and then in the larger arenas. Tough we do become expert "rock throwers"! Local political farm systems support the development of national candidates. Where do you think Sarah Palin came from? Was she groomed by a cabal of "New World Order" thinkers? Hardly! She started out as a school board activist! Hence patience over panic, planning over reaction, and intelligent action over protest wins the day!

Yet, most Christians hold to a "top-down" approach to political thought that deleteriously ignores grass-roots foundations. Result? The saints are marginalized as protestors with little if any bite. Indeed, if I had a dime for every sincere saint who said something akin to "I don't care about this local stuff . . . look at what Obama is doing to the nation" I would be a very wealthy man indeed.

When you add the varied conspiracy theories to the milieu, the saints are at a huge disadvantage. "Success" is deemed impossible in that even if some measured advance is noted "the conspiracy" either real or imagined will succeed in thwarting any meaningful advance. Hence local politics is seen as naive and without hope for promotion. Yet it will be local politics, state sovereignty issues, governors and business leaders that will determine the outcome of the Obama years, not Federal obsessions, international cabals, or elite effete billionaires!

A Dominion Attitude

A dominion attitude rejects defeatist notions and embraces long term biblical strategies which ensure a "little by little" conversion or defeat of entrenched political adversaries. Some of these strategies include:

1) Training explicitly Christian candidates in issues of civil polity, campaigns, and theology. This is paramount! You can't beat something with nothing!

2) Building campaign organizations that are not dependent on the party. That is building a self-sustaining entity at every level of campaign involvement. THIS IS IMPERATIVE! More Christian candidates have lost races due to their naive dependence on state party machines than any other single factor. The machine is NOT on your side! No exceptions! Build your own base, over successive elections and watch how effective you become as a power broker for Constitutional causes!

3) Training precinct committeemen for party service. Concentration is on trained Christians who look to control the executive committee and various other committees (finance, public relations, candidate recruitment etc.) with an eventual Christian party chairman that takes seriously his mission to win back and advance basic Christian cultural ideals.

4) Running races at local and state levels. That is zoning boards, city council, county offices, health boards, school boards, state representative etc. Start with the achievable and LEARN!

5) Involvement in vital peripheral organizations such as the Chamber of Commerce, Rotary Clubs, or start your own think-tank!

6) Discipleship of existing civil magistrates.

7) Committees of correspondence and phone/email/fax/blogging networks to bring public pressure to bear on various issues.

8) Using antithesis both in campaigns and marketing to help define the battlefield in the community. Politics is war by another means! Grow up! Remember Jesus called the scribes and Pharisees "whitewashed tombs and vipers".

9) After one local county party is sufficiently controlled, branching out into the contiguous counties within the same congressional district.

10) Encourage Christian independents to also run for non-declarative races (city council) and so as to raise up an alternative group of candidates that can assert pressures from outside the main parties.

11) Start your own business! Especially in an age when entrepreneurism is frowned upon by the Obamaites, what better way to resist and prosper than to start your own business!

Church Recruitment

The average church in America has membership of approximately 190 people. If each church represented on the SGI mailing list were able to activate 10% of their parishioners toward service in the civic realm, a great political force would arise. Now many a churchman decries political involvement. They claim we are not "saved" through politics! To which I agree! But one must ask the question for what end did Christ save us? Certainly he saves us from our sins and sanctifies us for an eternity spent with Him. Nevertheless we are not placed in this life to take up space, but to press His claims in every sphere of life. Politics is of importance because in this age it has become the chief battleground, the place of contest and the great engine of brutish state power. Our involvement in the body politic will be to make politics of less import through limited government power, greater personal freedom and responsibility, and finally emphasis on family renewal in Christ. In the end we work for a world free from Caesar that we may be free in Christ!

CHAPTER ELEVEN

Concerted Prayer and Proclamation

Given the foundations so far addressed in our narrative, it is paramount for the Church whether Catholic or Protestant to have joint proclamations of concerted prayers for our nation. In this regard I print two proclamations which can be utilized for "Tea Parties", corporate prayer meetings, or national proclamation. In this context the prayer for President Obama was personally delivered to the White House in April of 2009.

PROCLAMATION

Whereas: The providential history of mankind is covenantal in nature, comprised of Divine blessings for obedience to the Law-Word of God, and negative sanctions for transgression of the same, and under consideration of the historic precedent of public covenantal proclamations regarding the unlawful actions of civil magistrates established by John Knox in 16th century Scotland, the combined members and associates of Statesmen Global Initiatives have during the month of January 2009, conducted concerted and public prayer for the President of the United States, Barack Obama, along covenantal lines, having the Davidic imprecatory Psalms as our form and pattern.

This proclamation serves as a synopsis of our activity.

Resolved: To the end that the President of the United States, Barack Obama, fulfills his duties as the covenantal head of this nation along Biblical lines; we as Christ's ambassadors pray and proclaim blessing. That is, if the President executes his duties in a fashion that would not be tyranny to good works and would uphold the abiding validity of God's moral law as delineated in the Ten Commandments along with the justice-mercy ethic derived from the New Testament, we do declare that blessing, honor, and good success would be upon him, his associates, and policies.

Resolved: In that the President of the United States Barack Obama has thus far sought the codification of behavior condemned in the infallible Law-Word of God, specifically homosexual "marriage" and tax-funded state-sanctioned murder in the form of abortion, we as Christ's ambassadors proclaim negative sanctions. That is: if the President continues to hold in disdain the Law-Word of God by ratifying evil and by such ratification holds our lives as citizens of the republic in bondage to the same idolatry, we as Christ's ambassadors do declare that Barack Obama must now repent and cease from his cruel persecution of innocent pre-born babies and his tyrannical oppression of God's people who would not be part of his pro-homosexual agenda. If the President ceases not from his malicious cruelty, we then earnestly pray that his days in office would be few and another man take his office, and that the name of Barack Obama would remain a reproach to all succeeding generations of Americans.

AN INVOCATION FOR YOUR LOCAL "TEA PARTY" OR PUBLIC SERVICE

Almighty Triune God, in the name of Christ we approach your eternal throne. Our Father, we acknowledge your providence and transcendence, as the one who upholds all things by the word of his power, who is before all things and by whom all things consist. Lord Jesus Christ, we submit ourselves to your benevolent rule, for the earth is yours and the fullness thereof and your name is above all names. Thou art Lord of the nations.

We humbly entreat thy goodness on behalf of these United States of America. May your Crown and Covenant, your Law, govern our affairs with righteousness and equity. Establish us with pure and undefiled religion and may the everlasting gospel diffuse its heavenly light and spread Christian brotherhood, liberty, and peace from sea to shining sea. We pray for our national and state governments, that all branches and departments may be constantly filled with the wisest and best men. Men who fear God and tremble at your Word. For the fear of the Lord is the beginning of wisdom. May all legislative assemblies be granted thine assistance to reward and advance righteousness, even while abhorring and restraining wickedness. May the administration of justice be in the hands of men well qualified for their offices, men not given to bribery or perverse judgments, which would throw down the bridle and sanction of law. Lord, may our civil magistrates with one voice, establish and defend our Constitution, that we the people may know the blessings of good governance. Lord Christ be in our midst, direct and assist us, impressing our hearts with your fear that we may know your present and future blessings in reward for fidelity to your inscripturated will.

We repent for the myriad of sins which our Republic and our states have committed against your ways. We repent for the great holocaust of abortion wherein the voice of innocence has been so cruelly dashed by the hardness of our own hearts. We repent for the grievous burdens placed upon our people and injury inflicted to the family by excessive-tyrannical taxation. We repent for governments' appetite for living beyond its means and jurisdiction, thus mortgaging our children and our children's-children's future. God grant us forgiveness and grace to act in accordance with your will. May we be resolute and undaunted to establish uncorrupted morality, and justice for all men. Grant us the vigor to protect and defend life, the voice to herald liberty and the spirit of enterprise in the pursuit happiness.

Finally, we stand shoulder to shoulder with our founding fathers and declare that the rights of man come not from the generosity of the state, but from the hand of God. For such liberties we pledge our lives, our treasures and our honor, to preserve and defend the altar of Liberty. SO HELP US GOD!

Now to Him who rules all things according to his own pleasure and wisdom be praise, honor, glory, and dominion forever and ever, through Christ Our Lord AMEN.

Chapter Twelve

Conclusion

Take heart today. God is the sovereign over all. The last three elections have proven that a divided America exists. Yet even among the more traditionally "conservative" sectors of our nation, very few are self-conscience as to the immutable orthodox Christian and western ideals that built our great civilization.

As described in our preceding chapters these ideals are not amorphous or ill-defined in nature, but are instead robust concrete principles that have been and will again be transforming to all cultural pinions. What we proclaim are not nationalistic feel-good notions that herald a bygone era; but instead bedrock confessional Orthodox Christian thinking that touch economics, enterprise, government, ethics, education, and family.

What I encourage is more than resistance to the current statist-collectivist regime, but a commitment to deal with the endemic conditions which allowed our current malady to exist. In this light, we must engage corporate America, including some of the largest enterprises throughout our country. So too it is imperative to instruct Capitol Hill "staffers" as well as the myriad of allied think tanks in our nation's capitol. Our plans should take in the largest churches and seminaries in both Catholic and Protestant realms and also seek opportunities at various colleges and universities and even public high schools. The sports world is also an open and effectual door with many coaches that are allied with our vision.

Together in Christ we are engaged in a grand adventure for future generations of Americans! For those of you reading our short treatise, I hope that we can meet and join together to encourage a grass-roots restoration of our grand Republic. God bless you!

www.ingramcontent.com/pod-product-compliance
Lightning Source LLC
Chambersburg PA
CBHW020409290526
45785CB00005B/2476